The Kushite Prince AKINIDAD

:And the Roman Kushite War

By

Clyde A. Winters

Table of Contents

CHAPTER 1: Introduction

In this book we will discuss and review the inscriptions of Akinidad and explain his possible role in the Meroitic-Roman War and crown prince of the Meroitic- Kushite empire. Akinidad is one of the most egnimatic historical figures of Meroitic-Kushite history. Prince Akinidad is usually associated with parents King Terteqas and Queen Amanirenas on many Meroitic monuments.

Generally, Meroitic studies focus on broad aspects of Meroitic society and history. In addition, much of the discussion of Meroitic-Kush is done through the eyes of non-Meroitic people or archaeology. In this monograph we will use the traditional sources of Meroitic history plus Meroitic textual materials which provide us with a more concise undertsanding of one of the key figures in Meroitic history.

Most researchers believe that Akinidad was a ruler of Meroitic-Kush eventhough he is usually referred to as **paqar** in Meroitic textual sources (Welsby, 1996; Torok, 1997). Hintze believes that Akinidad was the ruler of Meroitic-Kush between 18

4

and 3 B.C.

Controversy has surrounded **Paqar** (crown prince) Akinidad since the discovery of the Hamadab I stela. Akinidad was the son of **Qor** (King) Teriteqas and **Kandake** (Queen) Amanirenas of Meroe.

On this stela there are over forty lines of archaic Meroitic script which many scholars believe records the Meroites side of the conflict with the Romans in 23 B.C. Although Dunham (1957,7) and Reisner (1923, 76), place the rule of Teriteqas and Amanirenas much earlier than the Meroites campaign against the Romans. But Griffith's (1917) interpretation of the Hamadab I stela appeared to indicate that this text might be the Meroitic side of the Roman-Meroite campaign.

Research indicates that Akinidad was closely connected with Lower Nubia. Griffith (1917) believes that Akinidad held the titles **paqar** (crown prince) and **pesato** (viceroy)[1] of Lower Nubia. (Hintze 1978,100)

We have come to know about Prince Akinidad from the association of his name with King Teriteqas and Queen Amanirenas in many Meroitic inscriptions. (Hoffman 1978, 86-94). The names of Amanirenas and Akinidad are associated on inscriptions from

5

Gebel Barkal, Dakka (Pelchis), Kawa and Meroe. (Hoffman 1977, 88-89) The names of Akinidad, Amanirenas and Teriteqas are associated with inscriptions from Gebel Barkal, Dakka and Meroe. (Hoffman 1977,88-89; Shinnie 1967, 43; Hintze 1959, 24-27)

Griffith (1917) published a study of the Hamadab 1 stela. Although Griffith (1917) could not read the stela word-for-word he was sure that the stela discussed a Meroitic campaign against the Romans. He based this conclusion on the decipherment of the word **arme**, in several places of the text which he assumed to mean :Rome.

The late dating of Teriteqas and Amanirenas in the chronology of Meroitic rulers is based on the Griffith (1917) reading of the Hamadab 1 stela. Hintze (1961) believes that the Hamadab 2 stela, which is badly damaged and unintelligible in many places, is a continuation of the alleged Meroitic discussion of the Meroites campaign against the Romans. Our decipherment of the Hamadab stelas and the other inscriptions of Akinidad from Meroe and Dakka, indicates that these stelas and graffiti are funerary inscriptions for Akinidad (Hamadab 2) and his brother Kharapkhael (Hamadab I).

The name Akinidad is written in several different ways in

the Meroitic inscriptions discussed below:

Akinidd	Hamadab 1
Akinid	Hamadab 2
Akinid	Dakka 2
Akidd	Dakka 1
Akided	Meroe 12(c)
Akini[d]d	Qasr Ibrim 1420

As illustrated above both in the Dakka 1 and Meroe 12(c) inscriptions the prince's name was written without the syllables **ni**. There was also irregularity in the writing of Queen Amanirenas name in Meroitic inscription 92, where the queen's name is written **Renas**. **Renas**, may be an abbreviated writing of **Arenas** (< Amanirenas), eventhough /**a**/ , is usually engraved in Meroitic inscriptions.

The people of Meroe, the Kushites had their own alphabet of 23 signs. This was a wonderful improvement over hieroglyphic writing which was made up of numerous ideographic and phonetic signs.

Francis Llewellyn Griffith, an Egyptologist was able to decipher the Meroitic script. Although Griffith deciphered

Meroitic, we were unable to read this writing because we did not know the cognate language.

Controversy has surrounded the origins of Meroitic. Scholars working on Meroitic do not believe Meroitic was an Afro-Asiatic language. Griffith and B.G. Haycock (1973), tried to read Meroitic using Nubian. Priese tried to read Eastern Sudanic in Meroitic; and Fr. Hintze attempted to compare Meroitic with the Ural Altaic languages. All of these attempts to read the Meroitic tablets failed.

In recent years researchers have been able to develop a grammar without being able to read Meroitic. The research of Hintze (1979) and Hoffman (1981) have made it possible for us to find the cognate language of Meroitic: Tokharian (Winters 1984 ,1989).

Hintze (1979) grammar of Meroitic provided the necessary material to compare Meroitic with other languages to find its cognate language. Hintze (1979) recognized three approaches to the study of Meroitic: 1) philological, 2) comparative, and 3) structural (i.e., the morphological-syntactical). The philological methods of Hintze (1979) was informed guesses based upon context.

Using the comparative method Winters (1984,1989,2012) was able to discover that Tokharian, sometimes referred to as **Kushana** was the cognate language to Meroitic. The discovery that Tokharian is cognate to Meroitic has led to the full decipherment of the Meroitic script. We can now read Meroitic using Tokharian.

Meroitic is an agglutinative language. The language includes both prefixes and suffixes--but suffixes are used extensively in the writing. The basic constituents of Meroitic is subject (S), verb (V) and object (O) in a simple declarative sentences. This agglutination and SVO order agree with other African languages.

The Meroitic script is a syllabic writing system. Each Meroitic consonant, except when followed by the vowel sign /i/, /o/ and /e/ represents the consonant sound plus the vowel /a/. There are four syllables in Meroitic **ne, se, te**, and **to** are represented by separate sounds.

Meroitic writing shows little resemblance to Greek writing. It has almost total agreement with Egyptian demotic. F. Hintze (1979) has noted that Meroitic writing is "strikingly similar" to Persian cuneiform in notating vowels and separation of words.

The Meroitic script is almost identical to many of the Kharosthi signs used to write Tokharian. It is interesting to

9

note that twelve of the Kharosthi and Meroitic signs have not only similar shape, but also the same sound.

Recognition of the cognate relationship between Meroitic and Tokharian allows us to read Meroitic, and give the Meroitic terms phonetic values (Winters,2012).

Using this information we have deciphered many Meroitic funerary tablets. The funerary inscriptions have the following order: 1) Invocation to Isis and Osiris the Meroites gods of the dead ; 2) Name of the deceased; and 3) obituary.

It appears from the inscriptions that Isis was responsible for giving the dead persons **Kha** , the right to leave for Paradise. Osiris, is the god who guides the deceased person's **h**, to one of the many after worlds mentioned in the Meroitic funerary stela.

In the Meroitic inscriptions there is constant mention of the **hi** 'body, spirit', the **Kha** 'the abstract personality', the **he** 'a shinning or translucent spirit soul; and the **Ba** 'soul'.

The **Kha**, existed within and without the human body. It would remain with the body until its flesh decayed, then it would either leave the tomb or hunt it.

In the archaic Meroitic inscription the deceased personage requested that the **Kho** be sent to **Hrph** , a place in the Meroitic after world. In the late Meroitic inscriptions the dead asked that they be sent to **henel, henepi** and **Bane** where the spirits lived. The Meroe dead often asked to have their **kho** , sent to **henepi** and the **Ba** to **Bane** (Winters,1999).

In the late Meroitic inscriptions the **Ba,** sometimes asked to remain at the grave or tomb. It appears that the tombs of important Meroitic personages were believed to be sites of effective talismanic power for Good.

Chapter 2: The Hamadab 1 Stelea

The most famous stela where Akinidad is mentioned is the
Hamadab 1 stela. This stela aws found in the town of Hamadab
which is located few miles south of Meroe City.

There are two stelas at Hamadab. They were erected at the
entrance of the Hamadab Temple.

The Hamadab 1 stela weighs 3 1/2 tons and is irregularly
shaped. It is 2.58m tall. At the top of the stela is 35 cm, while
at the bottom portion of the stela it thickens up to 40 cm. It
was published by Griffith (1917) and Villard (1959).

Hamadab 1 is believed to be the Meroitic record of the
Meroitic-Roman war (Grifith,1917; Torok, 1997; Villard;1959;
Welsby,1996). Torok (1997, 456) has hypothesized that
Hamadab 1 is the "triumphal inscriptions" of the Meroites war
with the Rome.

There are 45 lines ruled on the gritstone Hamadab 1. Forty -
two lines contain text and the last three lines are left blank.

An important scene formed the apex of the Akinidad stela that is now broken off. The remaining lower part of the scene shows

Hamadab Stela

the legs of six figures. The position of the feet indicate that
the figures were male and female. Griffith (1917) describes the
scene as follows:

> "On the left a woman with sandalled feet followed by a
> man barefooted confronts a god who wears the lion's
> tail; on the right the same pair confront a
> goddess.(Griffith 1917,163)

Griffith (1917, 163) has suggested that the male and female figures on the Hamadab 1 stela may represent a queen, and a prince, because the male's feet are bare. This may have been a symbol of "respectful inferiority". These personages are making offerings to a god and a goddess.

Below is the transliteration and translation of Hamadab 1 stela:

1. Amnirens ne . Qor e li ne kd(i) w-e li-ne. Yi-t[2] ni d b h e l-ne. Qor e y i ne ak-i[3].

2. Ñi d d ne pqr ñ. Yi ne. Pe s-t-ñ[4]. Yi ne Pqr ne qo ri ine se ne hrphel w-ne qe s̱-ne-a.

3. Rme yo s li-ne qe r-ne hrphel nea h[5] ro se-ne Bane[6] tm-o t-ne hrph e nea r si l-ne.

4. Qe s t[e]ne br sl-ne y-e ke di-ne kdi sl-ne ar s li-ne tk k-ne y e-mo qe-ne qe Bes wi.

5. Yerk i ne ar me-y sl h e-ne a d hi t[e]ne qe per-ne a br t[e] o-ne kdi...qo leb-ne ye.

6. H i ne ar b h ke pqr li-ne ye d o-ne qe e i net h e-o-a[7] ne-to o de B ne a bek B ne ẖs dl e d.

7. N̲ ro ne-l de-t[e] qo ne er o ñ-e-ne er o de bk t[e]ne e qo leb B h l-ne ye h k-ne ar o b el ne s̱ p t[e]ne qe-m[8] tone qo.

8. R ne hr k h el-ne -a h ro qe sl-ne-a t^{e}b e lh l-ne hr sh e E-ne qe s-ne n k to-ne a ro be ene a br s.

9. Ene ye keñ-i kdi s l -ne ar sl i ne...k-ne e ho qe ne qe bes wi-ne r k-ne sl t^{e}ne aro b ene.

10. An b i t^{e}ne he wite nea br h-ne m ni m so o-ne qo le B ne-a[9] lo t^{e}b s-ne neh k k-ne ho ine ne y.

11.T^e o r ne se i ho ste lo-a[10] br sl-ne se d-ne k n-ne sl-ne ar...sl ne h k-ne e mo qeqe b e.

12. S wi-ne ye r k ine ake s ne h k-ne se t^{e}l h ene añ añ[11] hi t^{e}ne-m r i t^{e}nea br k...k ñ im o-i qo.

13. Leb-ne a o t^{e}ne q s bl sne ye-t kb h i ne y qo l-ne h-ne al-e i ne qe s to-ne m e le el-e b nea br.

14. L-ne y ek...d-ne kdi se kers li-ne lk k-ne d qe b e s li-ne a kl lo o-ne el kb hi- ne ar ked ni.

15. ...lq e Bes ine hr-b[12] hi ne al e b so pe rt^e s qe s ne q o lh b wi-ne h hrph b h e w-o... m o.

16. Al e qe s wr d le i-ne lq s de b h ene s b...el b wi-to s-ne ye s bl-ne ne s s qo w nea.

17. ...lq-l p i-ne hl...l wi t^{e}l-ne ke yo s...e ho bl-ne k k-ne d d[13]ne...qo lo b ne...t^e s-ne ye.

18. S bl qe bes li si-ne s b, s-ne ml s wit^e li-ne qor ne-n

ene ne ye to-ne-a s̲.

19. ...e o or nem e ol s̲ amn k-ne p-n pk ne a i ro
ne...hrph i-ne b e ek...b lk wi h o ne qo le b ne ye o o.

20. L-ne y es b wit^e s ne-n h̲i w nea am k ok-ne yi ro h̲-ne m
d e wi nea ne s b ne kr...li-ne ar e.

21. H-a k i-ne i ne t^{e}ñ-a ene-t^e w wi b h l-ne sb-ne mek kl
nea d b el e h ene s̲ no qe-ne s b ne h ene s̲ no qe-ne s b-ne m dl
y b el... ne s̲ q....

22. Ñ̲ li nea d bl el h ne rm t^{e}ne qe s̲ li-ne lo li-ne i ke
l-ne s b ne s bl h l-ne e no wi lo ne w -l br-o.

23. P h e-a ne h̲...i no...r e h̲i-ne s b wi-ne ek t^{e}ne kdi se
w ne a br se w ne ye mo qe.

24. M qe eb es wi l-ne w k b t^{e}ne bo-ñ̲[14] pal h l-ne e-t^e w wi
lo ne s̲ m o li ne d s̲b el ine li-ne s̲ d e w ey ñ-ne h kdi.

25. At^e e t...k-ne w wi ke h i ne-l-ñ e ye k-ne-a b wi k h
ne wi p...a -ne w wi k e wi-ne l ro t^{e}ne li-n ñk ene w.

26. Li h̲i d b t^{e}ne-a sn t^{e}ne qe rk i sl w ah̲ r nea h̲i de b
w...wi-ne...m s Akinidd.

27. Qo-ne k q r li-ne ke s̲-to li-ne k q wi ek ene m no ne i
ne e qe-t^e h-n̲ ne-a-n t^{e}ne h̲ no.

28 T^e se ke-ne h̲ k ne-n li ne e qe m h-ñ k q r i li-ne ke s̲

li-ne-t^e b i-e ni d e b.

29. H e ne qor e s̲ i-ne nk h̲ bi h ne al rm ne h̲ hr lo sn ne ah ko ine ar r-l s.

30. S-ne kr-t^e ñ s-ne hr ph l-ne w s k-ne tk-m[15] ne sb ne kr t^e li-ne ar-m h no ke wi.

31. Q-n̲ d el t^e h s̲ i b h l-ne sb ne-b ek ene pe d bl e e h e-n el no qe-ne sb ne h̲ t^e y.

32. B e li-ne s̲ ho̲ s ñ li nea d bl e e h ne h̲ br e t^{e}ne qe h̲ e ine ho̲ li t-i-a ne s.

33. B ne s bl h ne l no wi t^{e}ne hrph ek l-ne h̲ wi d One i r h hi sb wi-ne.

34. E qe s wi m ne ek t^{e}ne k t^{e}ne kdi se w nea br se w ne ho̲ qe qe b e s wi l-ne w.

35. Pt^e t^{e}ne pe de ke se ke-ne hr kh-ne qo leb-ne w-t^e d e t^{e}ne-m k-ne wi-t^e p i de.

36. Lk ene qo-ne i... r ph enep bo li-ne ek k ...t^e de-t^{e}l e bk-ne-a[16] h i e ne pe.

37. Ke-ne wt^e de t^{e}ne-a s̲ Npte ne p i de...ke-ne sb ne r-a w h e li-ne pe-t.

38. H̲ ken o wi-net^e ñk ene-l br k-ne q r t^{e}ne el kb h-t-ne hb ene-l.

39. Sl-ne mk-t nea h̲ Ni-ne ar re s s-ne Amn k-ne ñtᵉ s ene ek-o.

40. P-ne k i d el ke-ne qo leb-ne h̲tᵉ de-b tᵉne sb ne tᵉ nk el h ene w wi-a wi ne-1.

41. O ro....tᵉne mi-n nk ine w e ne k i d b tᵉne a sn tᵉne qe r li s-1.

42. W ne-a s̲ r-a h i de-b h e wi-a great m-y-ñ.

Below is the translation of the Hamadab 1 stela.

"1. Amanirenas the Good. Give the monarch exalted Good. Give guide to merit (and) exalted Good. She will go donate a shinning Ba and Kha (to) live (forever). Give the monarch complete Good.

2. (She is to) give the glowing good bequeathal of her crown prince. Go bring (him) good. Bestow here protection on him. Go bring (here) Good. The good crown prince indeed leaves for the good rebirth. The good son Kharapkhael('s) superior renewal will (be) close at hand.

3. To witness from a distance the patron's departure. Indeed renewal to be give(n) to Kharapkhael. Now the Kha (is) to unlock the supporter('s) march to give the Ba Good.
(Here) to be reborn your Good (and) take aim at dignity. Now (he is) certainly indeed content.

4. Renew the son now. Bring the patron (into) existence. Give permission for its passage to obtain (for) the patron its conveyance to reflect on the (son's) revitalization. Give form to the making of Good. Bes[17] makes honor.

5. Go give homage to Good. Produce (a) considerable measure of (it for him). The Kha('s) bestowal--it gives the Khi (the body) a rebirth. The renewal Uplifts. It bears the commencement of merit...make the Restoration journey.

6. Go good Kha beget the Ba. The Kha proceeds (the Ba). The crown prince has departed on a journey. The bequeathal commences Good. The son go(es) for renewal. Bow in reverence (to the gods). Give the boon opening to manifest from a distance the offering. The good Ba it will mature. the good Ba to know (its) rising. Give the offering (now).

7. He is to unlock Good. Your almsgiving restores Good. Produce the commencement of Goodness. Evoke the commencement of mature almsgiving. Give the rebirth to restore the balance (between) the Ba and the living Kha. Give form to the boon. The Object of Supplication will commence to produce and give life to the Ba. The son implores to praise Good. It will make a restorat(ion) of (his) dynamicism.

8. Good indeed (is) dignity. It is obligatory to give a boon. Here the manifestation of the Kha will unlock and create his merit. Give loftiness to behold existence and dignity (for the) spirit body. Give renewal to almsgiving and his Uplift is obligatory (for) his rebirth. Open (up) the bestowal of Ba to sustain the patron.

9. The almsgiving is capable of this Revitalization. Give permission (for its) passage (to) consecrate Good. The exalted patron/son to beget (and) give...Give revitalize(d) soul existence and renewal Bes (oh) Object of Respect. The revitalized patron's rebirth to perpetuate the Ba almsgiving.

10. The Ba spirit leaves for rebirth. Give consent for the offering to sustain now the abstract personality of man. Measure the shinning. Measure the son's commencement of accession. (It) will give renewal to the good Ba. The solitary soul announces in a lofty voice the good son's passing. Give permission for the realization of the good soul to leave for (a new) existence.

11. Here indeed Good is to reach the son. Go solitary rich soul. (You) will dispatch suste(nance) and merit. Protect the good donation, (it) ask (for) permission for Goodness. Produce merit....Consecrate grand Good. Give (to) the Object of

Supplication a boundless renewal. Give (it to) the Ba.

12. Protect (this) Object of Respect on his journey (to renewal). Indeed give permission (as is) the Way for the patron to acquire grand Good. This Object of Supplication favor the elevation (of) the almsgiving (of) the Kha, the life spirit and body for rebirth. Go indeed now to sustain...Give permission for Good to reach and go open (up its) creation.

13. The restoration will commence the rebirth. Act patron to praise and adorn the new vivification. Give permission for the Ba and Kha (as is) the Way to form the living renew(al). Give the noble abstract personality of man leave to create Good. The patron's great dynamicism registers here, the gift of the Ba. Now (Oh God) sustain (it)....

14.Make living nourishment...the bequest is to gain and endorse understand(ing). (The) exalted (one) is to behold the realization (of) leav(ing) a legacy of renewal registered for the exalted patron's Ba. It (will) endure the dispatch of the commence(ment) of Good. The (Ba) gift desires going toward greatness, to beget and sustain shinning (Good).

15....l giv(ing) witness to Bes, is the Way to much dignity. The good body gives the noble living Ba favor. You indeed protect the good patron. Act to commence to behold the Ba (as an) Object of Respect. The Kha takes aim at dignity. The grand Ba gives guide to (its) opening....measure its beginning/rise.

16. Give the noble creation (of the) pleasing bequest here, (as is) the Way. Witness the patron's donation of the Ba and the Kha (as) almsgiving. Protect the Ba...The gift (of the) Ba takes pleasure in propping up the journey to protect the righteousness of the good patron. The renewed patron (will) guide it now.

17. ...] Act to be a foundation (as is) the Way to support...] your living honor. Spread (it) in the direction of the patron...give glorification for the soul. Give permission (for) the Object of Supplication a considerable donation of Good...Restore the good lovely Ba..t^e protect Good (and) give it form.

18. Bes the exalted, protects the law of renewal. (Give) atonement to the patron's Ba. Prop up the patron's spirit (for) exalted delight. The good monarch's almsgiving...gives form to Good. Vigorousness will be the patron's (destiny).

19. ...Give beginning to the release of reverence (Bes). Give the grand patron (of) Aman revitalization. He prays to take aim at Good...go unlock Good...take aim at dignity as is the Way.

Give the Ba nourishment...The Ba to uphold honor. The Kha to open (up) the restoration (of) Good. The good Ba begins the opening (up of Good).

20. Form the living manifestation of delight (for the Ba). It protects the good Khi. Guide Good now (to) the inner heart. Give permission for the acquisition of Good. Go make the unlocking of the (great) abstract personality of man. Measure the bequeathal of honor now. Protect the good Ba and dignity...Give rise to exalted Good.

21. His Kha ask permission (as is) the Way to come into being almsgiving. Guide (it) to much honor. The living Kha protects the considerable Good of the Ba. Resound now the donation of the Ba. Give the gift of the Kha's almsgiving to exist anew. The creator protects the good Ba. Make measure the offering of the Ba gift..in truth the patron act(s) to....

22. His exalted Good will praise the gift of the good Kha to witness mak(ing) the rebirth. The exalted patron to dispatch exalted good. Go give permission (for its) existence. Protect the good Ba and praise the living Kha. Give it honor now and dispatch Good. Guide (it) perpetually.

23. Pray the Kha will be given Good. h̲... go now...give

indeed the good body to protect the Ba and nourish Awe and (it) desires rebirth. Guide the son and direct Good to him. Guide good to the son. Give form to the vast creation(of Good).

24. Act to measure and give cover to the manifestation of living honor. Give permission to guide the Ba (to its) rebirth. (This) will swell-up praise (for the) living Kha. You give the guide to honor(ing) the good offering of the patron. Measure (indeed) the open(ing) of exalted good. Give (here) the piling up of the bequeathal (of) exalted Good. The exalted Good of the patron guides the bequeathal (of) exalted Good. The exalted good of the patron guides the bequeathal (of) exalted good. The exalted good of the patron guides the bequeathal to give (a new) existence to the grand Goodness (as is its) duty.

25. Give the path **t**...guide (him) to the realization of revitalize(d) honor. Go good Kha indeed give good (you) will (be) capable of (the) realization (of Good). Honor the Ba. Give permission for the good Kha to solicit honor...**a** Guide (to him) Good and Honor. Give permission for the Object of Respect to unlock indeed his exalted rebirth. God guides the almsgiving.

26. The exalted spirit body (of my son) gives much to the skillful rebirth. Renew the rebirth and go extend (it, so as) to

set in motion his guid(anc)e to learning. Good indeed now the spirit body offering (that) guides (him to) the boon...Good honor...measure and protect (it) Akinidad.

27. Give permission for (its) restoration. Indeed make exalted Good your revitalized patron. Give (him) permission (for) exalted Good. Make honor and sustenance his almsgiving now. (He) is capable now to go and give Good. You will make his Kha Good; and a grand rebirth now.

28.Here the son's grand revitalization is obligatory. His welfare give(s) exalted Good. Measure the renewal of his Kha, as is obligatory. Indeed (he) desires to leave. Give permission (for) exalted Good. Go to be satisfied with your exalted Good. The Ba go(es) to give illumination. Give the donation of the Ba.

29. Register the (Kha) of the monarch's son (as is) the Way grand God (at) this moment. The good and noble Kha to touch grand Goodness and dignity. The clever good offering to learn a glamorous Way. Indeed produce its protect(ion).

30. The new vivification to be his dignity. The new vivification aspires the gift of living dignity. Protect and guide the almsgiving to investigate his Good. The good pile of dignity is to be exalted Good. It is to produce much (Good) now.

Give (it) permission for honor.

31. Give here understanding as a good gift. Grand satisfact(ion) (for) the Ba and anointed living Kha. Grand Good to nourish the almsgiving. Bestow and donate the registration of praise. Give boon, he gives (this) gift now. The creator piles (up) grand Good existing this place.

32. Give the Ba exalted Good (and) protect the soul. The son's welfare will be exalted Good (as) the bequest. Register praise and give the good Kha grand support. Give the rebirth to make a grand renewal as is the Way. The exalted soul go(es) to arrange Good (for) the patron.

33. The good Ba protects and praises the good Kha. Indeed now honor the rebirth (of Kharapkhael) (he) aspires the gift of dignity to nourish the living. Give glory accession. Indeed go Kha. Go Kha anointed with Awe/Honor.

34. Give renewal and protect (his) honor. Measure the Good, to nourish the rebirth. Give permission (for) the rebirth to require the patron to guide now (its) sustenance. The patron guides Good to the soul's renewal. Make (and) give protect(ion) to the Ba (and) guide living honor to it.

35. Lay a foundation for the rebirth. Pray (for an) offering

of revitaliza(tion) for the origination (of my) son. The origination of dignity (is) obligatory (for the) recognition of the restoration. You guide to the restoration the offering of his rebirth. The object of supplication go(es) to pray to take pleasure (in this) offering.

36.Behold the almsgiving (of Amanirenas for) the good restoration...Indeed (Kharapkhael) aspires the bestowal of inflated exalted good to nourish k...here your offering to elevate (one) and give (much) perfection. Go give (it) boon and implore (the gods) for good.

37. You guide the revitalization (of) the offering (of the) rebirth. The son of good Napata go(es) to supplicate the offering...The revitalization piles (up) good. It indeed guides and gives the Kha exalted good. He implores (it).

38. Realize grandeur and the commencement of veneration. Give God almsgiving to sustain (this) object of supplication. Indeed act to desire the gift of rebirth. His good boon (to be) a large boon of generosity.

39. Here much merit and now grand shinning. This Radiance indeed beget(s) protection (for) the good patron Aman (the) revitalized. Your Good (Oh Aman) protects and nourishes the

commander.

40. Go make prayers (to God) (for the) gift of revitalization to be renewed. The restoration spreads much almsgiving (for) the rebirth to consecrate your Good. God's gift (a) boon of almsgiving to guide his honor, as an object of respect.

41. Commence to unlock...the rebirth of (our) God('s) good libations as is the Way. give guide to good (Oh Aman). (It) is obligatory to go and give rebirth to his Ba. The skillful rebirth of the patron's Ba indeed makes exalted indeed the patron.

42. Guide good to the son. His boon indeed goes (to seek) much almsgiving. Give great honor his boon. He is (to) live on."

Hamadab 1 tells us very much about the Meroitic religion. We learn that the Meroites were very interested in the deceased person living a life of exemplary Goodness. We also found out that this stela did not discuss the Meroites campaign against Rome.

The most interesting fact about this stela is the fact that the Meroites god Bes was mentioned as the protector of the spirits of Kharapkhael. Bes the dwarf god appeared during the Egyptian 12 Dynasty (2000-1790 B.C.) . Patrick (1972, 55) believes that Bes may have originated in the Sudan.

Bes wears lion or leopard skin . He was protector of the family and he presided over childbirth, and was on hand to drive away evil spirits. This suggest that Kharapkhael may have died during his early youth. This may explain the use of Bes as the guardian spirit of the Ba and Kha of crown prince Kharapkhael.

In line 26 of Hamadab 1 we find mention of Akinidad:

> "The exalted spirit body (of my son) gives much to the skillful rebirth. Renew the rebirth and go extend (it, so as) to set in motion his guidance to learning. Good indeed now the spirit body offering (that) guides (him to) the boon...Good honor...measure and protect (it) Akinidad."

In this passage we do not find Akinidad described a **paqar.** This suggest that Kharapkhael was the original crown prince, not Akinidad of King Teriteqas and Queen Amanirenas.

Griffith believed that **arme**, meant Rome. This group of Meroitic syllabic signs did not mean Rome. These letters represented four words **a ra m e** , or "Indeed he gives measure".

In summary, the Hamadab 1 stela is not about a battle against Rome, it is a recording of the death of the oldest son of

Teriteqas and Amanirenas, Kharapkhael. The text of this stela makes it clear in line 2, that Amanirenas:

> "(She is to) give the glowing good bequeathal (of) her crown prince. Go bring (him) Good. Bestow here protection on him. Go bring (here) Good. The good crown prince, indeed leaves for the good rebirth. The good son Kharapkhael('s) superior renewal will (be) close at hand."

This indicates that Kharapkhael was the original crown prince and that Akinidad only became crown prince as a result of the death of his older brother Kharapkhael. This death may have caused some political dissension in Meroe, since the death of Kharapkhael, may have made a brother of Teriteqas or Amanirenas eligible for the throne instead of Akinidad.

Chapter 3: The Travels of Akinidad

As mentioned earlier Akinidad is mentioned in many Meroitic inscriptions. Now that Hamadab 1, has been deciphered in its entirety we discover that King Teriteqas and Queen Amanirenas probably promoted Akinidad on many of their inscribed monuments to legitimize his appointment as crown prince of Meroe after the death of Kharapkhael. Teriteqas and Amanirenas therefore may have made travels to the Meroitic religious centers to attempt to find legitimization for Akinidad as crown prince.

Pilgrimages to Meroitic-Kushite holy places would have provided the public ample opportunity to see the new Crown Prince acting royal after he reached the age of maturity. These pilgrimages by Teriteqas and Amanirenas to religious sites in Meroe would explain the appearance of inscriptions bearing the name of Teriteqas, Amanirenas and Akinidad at many Meroitic religious sites.

The first mention of Akinidad as Crown Prince may be the Meroitic inscription, Meroe 12(c) (REM 0412) (Griffith ,376-378):

Teriq qe sne qor-o

Amnirens ne Kdke

Akided ine s̲ s̲-ne

t^{e}l-o ne.

The translation of the Meroitic inscriptions from Meroe City,

Meroe 12(c) is as follows:

"Renew Teriteqa(s) the good and nobel King.

The good Amanirenas the Queen.

The good Aki(ni)ded is destined (to be) King".

Akinidad also visited Dakka. The Dakka inscriptions give us

the first mention of Akinidad as **paqar**. In Dakka 1, we read:

Teriteqs qore ne Rens kdke ne Akidd pqr s̲k-te a br

sli ke de-to kdi s deto Wos...a br s ed k i d de

to...li a br sli ke de to-ne kdi sli ar e de to-a d-b

wi-ne w ke kt$_e$ ah m o r ne p el m o s ñ yi ah ro qe

de ti w-e̲ h̲.

The translation of Dakka 1, is as follows:

"Give Good to the monarch Teriteqas. Renas the good

queen. Akinidad the crown prince. The king will

originate (and) sustain the dynasty. Revitalize and

excite this offering. (It is Teriteqas') duty to

support the excite(ment) of the offering to
Isis. He sustains and protects the necessary path
to give leave to animate the offering...exalted.
He sustains the revitalized dynasty and originates
the bequeathal of Good. The duty of the dynasty is
to give rise awaken(ing) the donation (Teriteqas
and his family). It gives much veneration to guide
and originate the revitaliz(ation) of great
learning. Commence indeed to pray (for the) gift
of Good(ness). Commence his protec(tion). Go bring
(on) learning."

In Dakka 1, we find mention of both Teriteqas and Amanirenas
in addition to Akinidad. The decipherment of this inscription
makes it clear that at the time this inscription was written
Teriteqas had grave concerns about the stability of his **sli**
(dynasty). This is shown by the passage:

"He (Teriteqas) sustains the revitalized dynasty and
originates the bequeathal of Good."

This passage may have been written shortly before Teriteqas
departed from Meroitic-Kush to help the Egyptian rebels in the
Triacontaschoenus around 25 B.C. (Torok, 1997). Teriteqas may

have died suddenly during the champaign in Egypt because there are no other references to Teriteqas after Dakka 1 was written. Moreover by the time the Romans reached Pselchis/Dakka, the Meroite forces were led by Candace Amanirenas.

In Dakka 2, there is no mention of Amanirenas or Teriteqas. We therefore believe that Dakka 2, appears to have written sometime after Dakka 1, was written. By the time this inscription was written Teriteqas may have already died , and Amanirenas may have been Queen of Meroitic-Kush.

The Dakka 2 inscription was probebly written after the retreat of the Meroites from the Triacontaschoenus. It would appear that in addition to King Teriteqas being mortally wounded in the Meroitic-Roman War, Akinidad may have also been injured in the fighting before the Romans pushed the Meroites back to Dakka. Below we provide the Dakka 2, inscription:

> Akinid pqr ne wek... h i ne nm tone ke d d y h̲ ne p i h
> tro-l bl tk i d ne s ñ y sli rh tone s̲ lne k lne k sl
> eb wi r s ne i-t...e ro ne y i kene Wos be sr li .

The translation of Dakka 2, is as follows:

> "Akinida[d] the good crown prince to guide the
> nourishment...go offer alms to make obeisance to

vigorousness give permission (for) the considerable bequeathal
to bring great Good. Go pray the boon (of) righteous eminence. Go
investigate the giv(ing) (of) Good. The existence (of Good)
close at hand goes to consecrate the spread of dynamicism.

The living (Amanirenas) to carry Good. It is

obligatory (for the Ruler) to set in motion the cover
(of) honor. Go arrange the spread of Good....Give
opening to Good. Go make the origination Isis (of) the register
of much exalted good luck (for Akinidad)."

It would appear from this inscription that Akinidad may have
died in the city of Dakka. The grief over first Teriteqas death,
and then Akinidad's death at Dakka may explain the shaky style of
writing which characterizes Dakka 2.

The Dakka 2, inscription is not the only obituary of
Akinidad. It would appear that Hamadab 2, is the funerary stela
of the Crown Prince.

Text of the Hamadab 2 stela was published by Hintze (1961).
The stela had 35 ruled lines. The last three lines appear to have
been left blank. Much of the Hamadab 2 stela is badly damaged.
Entire lines of the stela have been deliberately destroyed, but
we can still read many of the legible lines of the text. Below

are the first 8 lines of Hamadab 2, which are very legible:

1. Er ne tm e y kwi-ne Akinid[d] ne pqr...i...y [ton]-ne
   e.

2. Wid tene en h tene tm e y ne....te-ne etr e B(a) h tene
   ar ke s̲.

3. Ed m n h te-ne...i net...ne e qe ti pl e ne tm e y ene-
   a br.

4. S wi-nw i r h e-ne kdi s wi-nw ar sl i we tk k-ne et eb
   tene tm e y o s wi net-m h tene p.

5. T tene sw ñ tene en ot ne tm e y ne s... r-i...sl i
   ne wt y tene tm e y s k k-ne p o.

6. Pl ne y o to-ne-a h ro b ne Npte ne i p ... l ... d ne
   er k i ne e de ... e d el w-ne i.

7. R h ne e r h p e b-ne p e ñ ...sl i ...st...li-ne-a d b
   e h we te s-ne.

8. Wi-m ol t-ne pe pe ne....ine s̲ ...i...ne k el m ne...a d
   h ne-m ro.

Below is the translation of this inscription:

   "1. Produce Good. Give form to the rebirth. It is obligatory
that this object of respect, Good Akinida[d] the crown
prince...go...give creation to (his) dynamicism".

2. Give honor and rebirth (to the patron). Command rebirth for the good **Kha** to give form to the rebirth....Give (him) rebirth. Give raise to the B(a) and Kha's rebirth. Beget now a revitalized patron/son.

3. He gives command for the **Kha**'s rebirth...go bow in reverence..Give good, go arrange the renewal and give righteous Good. (He) will sustain and give rebirth to almsgiving.

4. Protect the Object of Respect. The **Kha** indeed desires the almsgiving('s) protec(tion). The Object of Respect. Produce and protect exalted Good; to reflect on (his) revitalization. You command the revitalization to cover and give form to the rebirth. Commence to protect (his) honor. He bows in reverence to implore rebirth (for the) **Kha.**

5. He guides and protects the arrange(ment) of the rebirth. Command Good admiration give form to the rebirth of Good and protect...Go indeed...Go set in motion Good. Arrange guid(ance) to make the rebirth. Protect Good. Give form to the rebirth of Good. Give permission for revitalization (of Akinidad), commence entreaty (for this).

6. Righteous Good will bring the commencement of vigorousness. The **Kha** to unlock abundant good (for) good Napata.

Go implore....1...bequeath good. Give permission to go and produce Good. Give the donation....Command the bequeathal of the gift (of Goodness) to go to the Commander (Akinidad).

7. Indeed give Good to the **Kha**. Indeed the **Kha** gives entreaty for **Bane**. He (Akinidad) gives entreaty ...go consecrate...give here...will give the **Ba** exalted Good. Command to place Good on the patron/son.

8. His grand good is honor. Bestow (on him) a good honor...the Way, the King...go...good...give permission his good gift...he donates the **Kha** (as a) witness of his good."

This Hamadab 2, makes it clear that Akinidad probably never assumed kingship . This would explain why he is always referred to as **Paqar** (crown prince) in Meroitic inscriptions , rather than King.

Chapter 4: <u>Qasr Ibrim Stelea</u>

The final textual material relating to Akinidad comes from an unpublished stela found at Qasr Ibrim. This stela is is Qasr Ibrim 1420.

Researchers usually refer to Qasr Ibrim 1420 as the stela of Amanishaketo and Akinidad stela (Torok, 1997). But our examination of a photograph of Qasr Ibrim 1420 indicate that Amanishaketo is not mentioned on this stela.

Qasr Ibrim 1420 is a fairly large stela. This stela was broken and deliberately disfigured. The top of the stela is broken but a pair of wings were engraved in this area as evidenced by the tips of each wing remaining visible on Qasr Ibrim 1420 today.

Qasr Ibrim 1420 has a long inscription. Presently we find 37 lines of cursive Meroitic script on this stela. There were probably additional lines on this stela, because the stela is broken below line 37.

This stela indicates that Akinidad died while he was a prince. We can not publish a translation of the entire document but it appears that Qasr 1420 was a funerary stela.

As a result of the fact that this inscription is not published I will only quote from lines 1-4 of Qasr Ibrim 1420. Here we read:

1." He goes to prepare the renewal (and) protection of the abstract personality. Protect the prestige of the prince as is the tradition (and) vouchsafe the soul and honorable offering."

2. Produce revitakization of the Ba to leave a grand legacy (is) obligatory...vouchsafe and guide his abstract personality, may it go forth to praise his spirit.

3. The grand patron praises the Chief. Aman opens the shinning translucent spirit for rebirth. (There) will be eternal honor indeed for the prince.

4. "The good embarkation of Akinidad (to Paradaise) to will grant the patron a boon, (and) bring (him) eternal good".

These few quotes from Qasr Ibrim 1420 indicate that at the time this document was written Akinidad was recognized as both Chief and Prince. In this passage the Meroitic term wl was used to designate Akinidad as a prince, instead of pqr.

The term wl 'prince', was probably reserved for Meroite princes that held administrative responsibilities. In addition to notingg wl, on the Qasr Ibrim 1420 stela we also find use of wl to denote a prince in the inscriptions associated with the personage Arayesabkheqo, interned in pyramid N.36.

Qasr Ibrim 1420 is the only textual evidence where Akinidad is referred to as w-ne 'Chief'. This suggest that at the time Akinidad died he was recognized as the leader of government at Qasr Ibrim. This would have been an important post for Akinidad, given the strategic location of Qasr Ibrim as a major center of culture, commerce and trade . To understand the destruction of Qasr Ibrim 1420, we must remember some of the events associated with the Meroitic-Roman War.

In 24 B.C. Roman forces were sent to fight in Arabia. According to Pliny and Strabo the Meroite-Kushites sacked Aswan and destroyed the Roman statues at Philae (Torok, 1997; Welsby, 1996).

In response to the Kushite expedition, Gaius Petronius with a force of 10,000 infantry and 800 horses pushed the Kushites back to Pselchis. Strabo (17.1.53) mentions the fact that the Meroites were led by a Candace.

The Romans and Kushites, according to Strabo began peace negotiations at Dakka in 24 B.C.. The negotiations failed, and the Romans puched their forces deeper into Meroitic-Kushite territory as far as Sara. They established forts at Qasr Ibrim (Torok, 1997; Welsby, 1996).

Akinidad was probably killed in 24 B.C. Strabo (17.1.54) mentions that the Candace's son . This son of the Candance was probably Akinidad.

We know that Akinidad was in Dakka on two occasions, once with Teriteqas, and later only with Amanirenas. In Dakka 2, we discover that Akinidad died at Dakka. This is most interesting because, the Romans pushed the Meroites back to Dakka in 24 B.C.

If Akinidad had been wounded outside Dakka, Amanirenas may have stopped in the town to obtain medical treatment for her son. After Akinidad died in the town, Amanirenas may have withdrawn from peace talks and continued the War.

If these events occurned , Amanirenas probably had a the Qasr Ibrim 1420 stela erected in Qasr Ibrim, to honor Akinidad who had served as the Chief of the city before the Meroitic-Roman War. The Qasr Ibrim 1420 stela was probably defaced and broken during the Roman occupation of Qasr Ibrim to show their contempt for the Meroites.

The Meroites resisted Roman occupation. By 22 B.C., the Meroites retook Qasr Ibrim from the Romans. In 21 B.C., a peace treaty was concluded between Augustus, and Meroite envoys on the Island of Samos.

Conclusion

In conclusion, our decipherment of Hamadab 1 make it clear that this tablet dose not record the Meroitic war with Rome. It is also clear that Akinidad never became king.

In Temple M250 at Meroe City there is a cartouche of Akinidad. Here Akinidad stands before a god probably Amun Re (Torok, 1997, 458).

Although Akinidad is wearing princely attire including the plain princely diadem. Torok (1997) assumes that Akinidad must have become King (Torok, 1997, 458). He reasons that Akinidad became King because the iconographic representations in Meroe City , was usually reserved exclusively for the "actual ruler who thus recieves legitimacy and power for the god" Amun (Torok ,1997, 459).

The textual evidence makes it clear that Akinidad remained a **paqar** until his death at Dakka in 24 B.C. This ceremony at Meroe City probably revolved around Akinidad's induction as "co-regent" of Meroitic-Kush.

The evidence of the Dakka 2 inscription and Hamadab 2 indicate that Akinidad probably died during Amanirenas rule of Merotic-Kush. After Teriteqas was killed during the Meroitic-Roman War, Akinidad may have become recognized as King, but without official succession, and his untimely death at Dakka, he remained until his death officially Crown Prince. This would explain our inability to find any evidence of Akinidad being recognized as anything more than a **paqar**, rather than a qore.

Although we can positively maintain that Akinidad probably never assumed the throne in the Meroitic Sudan, we still have to answer the question where was Akinidad buried? Most Meroitists agree that the pyramids of King Teriteqas and Queen Amanirenas are located at Gebel Barkel. Another pyramid which is "chronologically attached" to these pyramids is Bar.5 (Reisner 1923 ,60).

The Bar 5 pyramid has the type -form analogous to the Beg. N.14 and Beg. N.21 pyramids which are assigned to King Teriteqas and Queen Amanirenas respectively. (Reisner 1923,60) Reisner found a male in this pyramid. This male lacked a crown of uraeus. This led Reisner (1923) to assume that this male never became King. Given the analogous nature of Bar. 5, and the Bar.4 and

Bar. 9 pyramids suggest that this may be the pyramid of Akinidad who never became ruler.

The death of both Akinidad and Kharapkhael probably led to Amanirenas assuming the role of ruler at Meroe until her death. This meant that no direct male descendant of Teriteqas took over the throne after his death .

During the rule of Teriteqas two new developments appear in Meroitic succession. These developments include the close association of the first wife of the king and their eldest son on many monuments. Hakem (1981, p.304) has suggested that some form of co-regency may have existed during this period in Meroe, because at the death of the king the queen became the reigning Candace .

The second major development in Meroitic civilization may have been the rise of a system of "strict direct succession". This succession called on the eldest son of the first wife of the king to assume the role of crown prince.

There appears to have been a high mortality rate among Meroite children. This high mortality rate may explain the possible emphasis placed on naming a crown prince before the death of the Meroite King by several of the queens that followed

Amanirenas including: Natekamani, Amanitore and Sherakaror. The sons of these queens appear to have had a high mortality rate.

For example, Amanitore is depicted with several different crown princes on buildings her and Natakamani built . It would appear that Arikankharer, Amanitore's eldest son, died and was succeed as crown prince by Arikakhatani, who is depicted on several monuments with the queen in Jebel Barkal and Naga. But it would appear that he also died and his younger brother Sherakaror was named crown prince. (Arkell 1955, pp.163-64) Sherakaror ascended the throne after his parents.

The sucession system created by Teriteqas was probably not recieved well by the Meroites. The anger caused by Akinidad's designation as **paqar** crown prince may explain the destruction the Hamadab 2 stela which is his funerary text. His death also marked a period of considerable anxiousness among Meroitic queens concerning the succession of the **paqar**.

It would appear from the historical evidence that when Teriteqas came to the aid of the Egyptian rebels in 25 B.C., he underestimated the military might of the Romans. This would explain the defeat of his army and eventual death during the campaign.

As a result of the Meroitic-Roman War we will never know what kind of ruler Akinidad would have become if he had not died at Dakka. But we can say that Akinidad never became King, he died as Crown Prince of Meroe.

REFERENCES

Adams, W.Y. 1976. "Meroitic North and South". Meroitica 2,Berlin
:Akademie-Verlag.

Arkell,A.J. 1955. A History of the Sudan. Wesport,Conn.:
Greenwood Press Publishers.

Brooklyn Museum,1978. Africa in Antiquity:The Arts of Ancient
_____ Nubia and the Sudan. Brooklyn,N.Y.: The Brooklyn Museum.

Dunham,D. 1950-62. Royal Cemeteries of Kush. Cambridge Mass.
Published for the Boston Museum of Fine Arts. Harvard
University Press. Vols. I-Iv.

Griffith, F.L.1911. Karanog. The Meroitic Inscriptions of Shablul
_____ and Karanog. Philadelphia: Eckley B. Coxe Jr Expedition to
Nubia. Vol.VI.

Griffith,F.L. 1917. Meroitic Studies III. Journal of Egyptian
_____ Archaeology, 4, .

Griffith,F. Ll. 1917 . Meroitic Studies IV. Journal of
_____ Egyptian Archaeology , 4 ,159-173.

Griffith,F. Ll. 19 . The Meroitic Inscriptions. Journal of
_____ Egyptian Archaeology, , 376-378.

Hakem,A.A. 1981. The civilization of Napata and Meroe. In

General History of Africa ,(London: Heinemann) ,278-297.

    Vol.2.

Haycock, B.G. 1978. "The Problem of the Meroitic Language",

    Occasional Papers in Linguistics and Language Learning,

    no.5: 50-81.

Hintze,F. 1959. Studien zur Meroitischen Chronologie und zu

    den Opfertafeln aus den Pyramides von Meroe. Berlin:

    Akademie-Verlag.

Hintze,F. 1961. Versffentlichten Meroitischen Inscriften.

    Kush, 9, 278-282.

Hintze,F. 1978. The Meroitic Period. In Africa In Antiquity:

    The Arts of Ancient Nubia and the Sudan. (Brooklyn,N.Y:

    Brooklyn Museum),89-105.

Hintze, F. 1979. "Beltrage zur Meroitishen Grammatik",Meroitica

    3, Berlin: Akademie-Verlag.

Hoffman,I. 1978. Beitrage zur Meroitischen Chronologie. St.

    Augustin: Verlag Des Antropos-Instituts.

Hoffman, I. 1981. Material fur eine Meroitische Grammatik.

    Veroffenthchungen der Institute fur Afrikanistik und

    Agyptologie der Universitat Wien, No. 16. Wien.

MacIver, D.R. and Wooley, C.L. 1909. Areika. Philadelphia

University Museum. Philadelphia.

Millet,N.B. 1969. <u>Meroitic Nubia</u>. Yale University, Ph.D.
    Dissertation.

Patrick,R. 1972. <u>All Color Book of Egyptian Mythology</u>. London.

Reisner,G.1923. The Meroitic Kingdom of Ethiopia. <u>Journal of
    Egyptian Archaeology</u> 9, 34-77.

Shinnie,P.L. 1967. <u>Meroe: A Civilization of the Sudan</u>. London:
    Thames & Hudson.

Torok, L. 1997. <u>The Kingdom of Kush: Handbook of the Napatan-
    Meroitic Civilization</u>. New York: Brill.

Trigger, B.G. 1970. <u>The Meroitic Funerary Inscriptions from
    Armina West.</u> New Haven, Philadelphia.

Villard, Ugo Monneret de. 1960. Incrizioni della Regione di
    Meroe. <u>Kush</u>, 8, 93-113.

Welsby, D.A. 1996. <u>The Kingdom of Kush</u>. London: British Museum

Windekens van, A.J. 1941. <u>Lexique etymologique des dialectes</u>.
    Louvain.

----------------.1979. <u>Le Tokhrien confronte avec les autre
    Langues Indo-Europeenes</u>. 2 vols. Louvain.

Winters, C.A. 1984. "A note on Tokharian and Meroitic".<u>Meroitic
    Newsletter</u>, no. 23: 18-21.

Winters,C.A. .1988. "The Dravidian and Manding substratum in
    Tokharian". Central Asiatic Journal, 32 (1-2): 131-141.

Winters,C.A..1989. "Chiekh Anta Diop at le Dechiffrement de
    l'ecriture Meroitique", Revue Martiniguaise de Sciences
    Humaines et de Litterature, no.8: 141-153.

Winters,C.A.1990. "The Dravido-Harappan Colonization of Central
    Asia". Central Asiatic Journal, 34 (1-2):120-144.

Winters,C.A..1991. "Linguistic Evidence for Dravidian influence
    on Trade and Animal Domestication in Central and East
    Asia",International Journal of Dravidian Linguistics,
    20 (2): 91-102.

Winters,CA. .(1998a). Meroitic Funerary text: Temple architecture and
    mortuary practices, InScription: Journal of Ancient Egypt,1 (1), 29-33.

_____.(1998a). Meroitic Funerary text: Stelae and funerary tables,
    InScription: Journal of Ancient Egypt,1 (2), 41-55.

Winters,CA (1999). The inscriptions of Tanyidamani. Nubica et Ethiopica IV \
    V, 355-388. http://www.scribd.com/doc/91808168/The-Inscriptions-
    of-Tanyidamani

Winters,CA. 2012. Meroitic Language. Scribd:
    http://www.scribd.com/doc/112999049/Meroitic-Language

VOCABULARY

Below is the vocabulary of the Meroitic terms from the
Akinidad text discussed in this paper.

A

ς2 **a**, he,it, to, ; masculine particle form .

   a,the ,intensive prefix .

ϡς2 **ah̲**, to learn .

ℛϡς2 **amn**, Amon

Ζς2 **ak**, completes,to learn, to teach, complement,supplement.

+Ζς2 **aki**, acquire knowledge.

ϟς2 **al**, noble

ϡς2 **am**, himself,soul .

ℛς2 **an̲**, spirit; **an̲an̲** , considerable spirit.

ζς2 **ap**, ancestor, father

ως2 **ar**, to bring out, produce, beget, arise .

+ως2 **ari**, manifestation, affirmation, revelation, apparition.

�ως2 **aro**, long (of time), olden, perpetual .

ς2ᘭως2 **aro-ne**, perpetuation, perpetuity, duration .

𝒦ς2 **aq**, replenish, to lead, complete, supplement .

ⲩⲱϚⳆ **art,** praise .

ⳆϚⳆ **at,** path , down the path .

ⲱⳆϚⳆ **atr,** hero .

E

Ϛ **-e,** singular nominal accusative .

   e, give ,vouchsafe, favor; (2) command ; (3) register .

ϚⳆϚ **e-ne,** alms giving ; grant a boon.

     e-ne, generosity, bestowal, contribution .

ⲓ4ϚⳂϚ **e-net**[e], 'your almsgiving'.

ⲓ4Ϛ **e-t**[e], you give; give you.

ⳠⳠϚ **ey,** give existence.

ⲖϚ **eb,** cover .

ⲌϚ **ek,** nourishment .

ⳝϚ **el,** gift.

   el, to produce, to call; **el-ne,** manifestation,revelation,

       prosperity .

ⳝϚ **em,** to teach, to instruct .

ϚⳆϚ **ene,** commander .

ⲌϚ **ep,** cover .

ⲭϚ **en,** command, punish .

ⲱϚ **er,** produce, evoke .

VII⟨ **es**, manifestation .

   es, well and good, good welfare, agreed, granted .

ᴗ⟨ **eto,** out here, out; way,route, road, path .

I

✝ **i**, go, goes, leave .

  i, this, these, those .

  i-, intensive prefix .

  -i, sign used to form agent nouns, e.g., **ot** 'to admire', **ot-i**
     'admiration' prestige'.

𝑉✝ **ib,** make .

𝟕✝ **ih̲,** (to) the spot.

𝟑✝ **i-m,** s/he goes, it goes .

  im, reach, do , make, act, attach .

  im, memory, remembrance, recollection .

⟨2✝ **ine**, the Way, within, according .

�7✝ **it**, it goes, go arrange .

O

| **o**, start, begin, commence ; ⟨2| **o-ne** commence.

  o, reaching .

ᔕ𝑙 **o-ne**, accession .

𝑙 **ol**, grand .

ᔕᔓ𝑙 **omne**, the acquisition .

ᖇ𝑙 **on**, to commence, to set about; to stay, to wait for .

ᔕ𝑙 **one**, touching from afar .

    one, acquisition, obtainment, procurement .

ᴣ𝑙 **ot**, admiration, prestige, esteem .

ᴢ𝑙 **od**, admiration; **od-o** 'admirable' .

Y

||| **y**, to make, to bring, to form .

    y, (its) leave, existence

ᔕᒾ||| **y-ne**, reach , achieve, attain, catch .

ᔕᒾ||| **ya**, go (to) .

ᔓᔕ||| **yem**, I am.

ᔕ||| **ye**, is capable (of this/that) .

ᔕᒾ╇||| **yi-ne**, to progressively.

𝑙 ||| **yo**, bow to, tender to .

    yo, and .

    yo, in the direction (of) .

ᴣ ||| **yt**, is capable (of) .

W

𝓑 w, to guide, to conduct, to lead, to drive , guidance ,direct.

Ϛ2𝓑 w(a)-ne, chief, commander,conductor; stewardship,
      directorship .

Ϛ𝓑 w-e, give escort.

wϚ𝓑 wer, purification .

VIIϟ𝓑 wos, Isis .

+𝓑 wi, to honor,guidance ; wi-ne honor, respect, Awe .

ℤ+𝓑 wid, to be in accord,to allow, to grant,to accept .

Ϛℤ+𝓑 wide, delight (149).

Ɔ Ϛ2+𝓑 wi-ne-t, your object of respect .

Ɔ𝓑 wt, put, place, sit; wt-o 'placement, disposition' .

Ɔ+𝓑 wit, to be in accord, to consent, to agree , to delight;

Ϛ2Ɔ+𝓑 wit-ne, pleasure, luxuriousness, contentment, joy .

I4𝓑 wt^e, consent.

ℤ𝓑 wd, put, place, set .

w𝓑 wr, purify.

B

Ʋ b, also .

  -b, abundance .

Ϛ2Ʋ b-ne, abundantly .

ᵛ **B(a)**, the united concept of the body and spirit body .

ϛ2ᵛ **B(a)-ne**, the good B(a).

ϛᵛ **be**, encounter ,accord, catch, catch up to .

ϛ2wϛᵛ **ber-ne**, confer, delegate, transfer .

ϛwϛᵛ **bere**, to raise (again) .

Ⅷϛᵛ **bes**, Bes, the Meroitic god of childbirth.

+ᵛ **bi**, today, actual, day moment .

ⰀᵛⰀ **bk**, ripen,mature ; **bk-ne**, perfection, maturity, ripening.

ⰀᵛⰀ **bl**, to praise, law , righteous .

ϛ2ⰀᵛⰀ **bl-ne**, righteousness .

ᴜᵛ **bo**, inflate, swell .

wᵛ **br,** to sustain, to bring, to bear, to support, to sustain .

ϛwᵛ **bre**, fault, mistake, blame .

Ⅷᵛ **bs**, protection .

P

ⱬ **-p**, imperfect prefix .

 p, beg, entreat, supplicate, pray ,solicit,supplicate .

ϛ2ⱬⱬᴠ hp **p-ne**, implore, beseech, entreaty .

ⱬ **p**, the foundation (of) .

ϛ2ⱬ **p-ne**, the foundation .

Ⰰϛ2ⱬ ⱬϛ2Ⰰϛ2 ⱬwϛ2+Ⅷϛϛ2 ϛϛ2� :

ᏚᏃ pe, implore .

ᏃᏚᏚᏃ ᏤᏚᏫᏓᏃᎶᏂᏚᏃ ᏓᏫᏆᏃᏚᏫᏣᏚᏃᏚᏃ ᏚᏃᏚᏃᏆᏫᏯ ᏚᏫᏞᏚᏃᏚᎤ

wᏚᏤ per, support .

 per, to boast, to praise ; **per-ne** 'adulation, glorification,
 grace, rapture, approbation.

ᏃᏚᏃ pet, reverence.

ᏃᏚᏃ pe-t, he implores (it).

ᏑᏃ **pl**, righteous .

ᏇᏃ ph, with the intention, to aspire .

ᏇᏃ ph, ripen, mature, decay .

 ph, to aim, to take aim .

ᏄᏃ p<u>s</u>, guard, protection (to the) .

ᏫᏃ pk, to aim, to take aim .

ᏦᏃ pq, fashion, make .

ᏃᏃ pt, to praise .

M

Ꮞ m, great, ; measure .

Ꮞ -m-, demonstrative pronoun he,his .

ᏫᏚᏤ med, unlock .

ᏓᏤ mi, rain, libations, imbibition, to drink .

 mi, injure .

▽ʒ mh, grand, great .

Ʒ ʒ mk, grand, great, considerable,much, many, various .

ʒʒ ml, under the influence, spirit, soul, heart ;   ml-o

　　　　'spiritual' .

ℝ+ʒ mi-n, good libations.

lʒ -mo, to be.

l4ʂ2ʒ ma<u>n</u>, month, moon.

l4ʒ mt^e, unlock, to open.

wʒ mr, unlock .

　　　mr, hand .

ɔʒ mt, break open .

ɔʂʒ met, release .

|||ʂʒ me-y, 'considerable measure'.

ℝʒ||| m-y-<u>n</u> , 'he is (to) live on'.

N

ℝ -n, singular normative plural .

　　　n, good .

　　　n, only .

ʂℝ ne, good ; ɔʂℝ **ne-t** 'your goodness' .

ʂℝ ne, in truth .

ʒʂℝ ne<u>h</u>, passing away, fade (away).

ᎫᏒ -ne, good, welfare; third person pronoun .

ᏒᎫᏒ ne-n, in truth, good.

ᎫᏃᎫᏒ nea, now .

ᏃᏙᎫᏒ nebk, in accord with, in agreement with .

ᏈᎫᏒ nei, in truth .

ᏃᎫᏒ nek, god .

ᏛᎫᏒ nem, bend, incline, reverence.

ᏚᎫᏒ net, bow in reverence .

ᏈᏒ ni, the shining, to shine, to illuminate, vividness

ᎫᏃᏈᏒ ni-ne, radiance, incandescence,brilliance .

ᏃᏒ nk, god , ᏚᏃᏒ **nk-t** 'your god' .

ᏛᏒ nm, to bend, to incline; ᏈᏛᏒ **nm-i** 'bowing, lending,obeisance
.

ᏬᏒ no, Now! .

ᎫᏃᏃᏒ np-ne, human being .

ᏜᏃᏒ npte, Napata .

(ᏬᏒᏜᎫᏒ nepteno) Hypothetical " to praise and direct its
start".

ᏃᏚᏒ ntk, the lord .

     ntk, bow in reverence .

N

x̲ n, good ??? .

-n, third person suffix 'he, his' .

ᏧᏔx̲ n-ne, his good .

_____ n-ne , goodness;to manifest, to show .

Ꮝx̲ nk, now .

ᏚᏴx̲ nl, penetrate, to conceal, to retire; n̲l-ne 'departure,
        parting ,emigration, embarkation .

ᏴᏴx̲ nt, honor, bow in reverence, veneration, piety ;homage ,
        worship, genuflect .

R

r(a), certainly, indeed .

w -r, verbal ending, e.g., s̲r 'king' .

ᏰᏧw ret, union, to unite, reconcile, reunite .

ᏬᏧw reto, inclination .

✝w ri, abandon, leave, send off .

    ri, surrender all claims .

Ᏸ✝w rit, to look, to search, to desire .

Ꮢw re, to , into, by, at.

Ꮝw rk, extend.

Ᏽw rm, touch .

Ᏽw rm, to touch, to witness;ᏧᏕᏽw **rm-ne** 'palpation,

manipulation'.

/ɯ ro, to withdraw, unlock, to open, to set .

ʙ̥ɯ rq, to cover, to escort .

Ⅶ/ɯ rs, to spread, to extend .

L

ƨ-l, termination particle, e.g., ƨ/ƨ lo-l solitary.

ƨ l, to be.

ʕ2ƨ l-ne, to exist, living .

   l-ne, suffix .

ʕƨ le, here , give .

2ʕƨ Ⅴʕƨ lep/leb, the balance, head, equality ;

       ʕ2Ⅴʕƨ **leb-ne** the restoration.

li, feeble .

+ƨ li, to be exalted ; **li-ne** 'the exalted' .

   li, departs ; **li-ne** 'transmittal' .

▽ƨ lh, to behold, to see , **lh-to** 'thou to behold' .

   lh, a distance, separate, distinct .

ʀ̣ƨ ln, to be settled, to be firmly established .

/ƨ lo, offering; solitary, lonely .

   lo, to send, send out, transfer, convey, dispatch .

ꝫlʓ lok, (from) [a]far .

ꝫlʓ lot, grave, hole, pit, opening .

ꝫʓ lk, to behold.

ꝫʓ lp, to be left, to stay ?????

ꝫʓ lq, to witness, to see, to be; **lq-ne** witness .

ꝫʓ lt, decline .

+ꝫʓ lwi, glory, well known

H

ꝛ **kh** , the kha, the abstract personality of man .

   kh,great, to offer boon/alms, favor, request .

ꝛꝛ **kho**, the Kho ,a shinning or translucent spirit soul.

+ꝛ **khi**, the Khi, the body, external body, spirit .

wꝛ **khr**, dignity .

ꝛwꝛ **khrp**, itself .

ꝛꝛwꝛ **khrpkh**, (1) take aim at dignity;(2) mature dignity;(3) to
                 aspire, dignity.

ꝛꝛwꝛ **khrpkh-n**, the good Harapah (a place) .

Vⅼⅼꝛ **hs**, just, justly, exactly .

<u>H</u>

ʓ <u>h</u>,great, grand .

ꝙʓ <u>h</u>-ne, abstract personality of man .

ऽ५ई **hel**, support .

+ई५ई **heli**, merit .

ऽई **hl**, to bear, to support, to tolerate .

ई/ई **ho-l**, soul .

wई **hr**, bear, endure, stand, tolerate; scatter ; dignity,

prestige, esteem, repute, **hr-o** 'reputable' .

wई **hr**, to smile, to laugh .

VII ई **hs**, to know.

ᒕwई **hrp**, himself, oneself, to be directed towards .

ठई **ht, to pour out, to spread, dispense .**

ᔔई **hto**, arise, come into being; **hto-ne** 'materialization,

phenomenon realization, existence, reality .

S

५२VII s-ne, new vivification .

    s-ne, prop up .

    s-ne, patron .

ईVII s-l, king .

VVII sb, heap, pile, piece, bit .

    sb, (1) cover;(2) rub with ointment, coat ;(3) anoint ??? .

ईVII sl, bring, set in motion, to leap over, to lead, to hop;

consecrate, dedicate .

ϚꝛᶴVII sl-ne, merit .

sl-ne, harmony.

+ᶴVII sli, dynasty, order.

+VII si, to be satisfied, satisfying, happy; **si-ne**, contentment,
satisfaction, atonement .

ℛVII sn, clever, skillful .

ധᗱVII sor, Osiris .

ꝛVII st, rich .

/4VII st^e, rich

VII s, from .

S

ᶾ sha, the king, patron .

Ϛꝛᶾ sha-ne, coming, approaching, close at hand, fated destined .

ᶾ+ᶾ sim, abode, house .

ᶾ sh, spirit body .

ᶾᶾ sm, refuge., equal .

ᶾᶾ sk, to remain , stay; sk-t^e 'you will remain'.

Ϛꝛᶾ sne, merit, uplift .

ϚꝛϚꝛᶾ s-ne-a, close at hand; (2) coming, approaching; (3) fated
disputed.

/ᶾ so, is alive, lives , life .

ᴣꙅ st, exaltation .

K

Ꙇ k, to be necessary, to be obligatory .

ꕚꙆ k-ne, revitalized .

   k-ne, realization .

   k-ne, object of supplication .

ꙆꕚꙆ kak, to know, to understand, to shout to send;ꕚꙆꕚꙆ **kak-ne**
                knowledge, recognition, cognizance .

ᐱꙆ kb, desire

ꕚꙆ ke, revitalize, to grow, to come ; **ke-ne** revitalization .

ke, permission, proceed, in front, suffix of reinforcement .

ꕚꙆ ke, act, give, spread ;ꕚᐺꙆ **ke-ne** the origination .

ꙥꕚꙆ ed, to bear, to support, to sustain, to resound, to
          reverberate .

ʁꕚꙆ ken, to realize .

ᴣꕚꙆꕚ ꕚʁꙆ kene/ kenet , revitalization .

ʑꕚꙆ kel, resound, endure, tolerate, lead .

ᐁⅼⅼwꕚꙆ kers, to know, to be aware.

ᴣꕚꙆ ket[k], to gladden, to cheer, to wish, to desire .

ꕚᵹⅼᐺꕚꙆ kete-ne, ascent, elevation .

ʑꙆ kl, bear, endure, tolerate .

Iⵠ ko, glamorous.

ⵞⵒⵧⵠ kh-ne, cognizance, recognition.

Iⵞⵠ kt°, arise , stand up, mount;(2) originate, spring up, begin

materialize.

wⵠ kr, dignity .

ⵥⵠ kd, merit

ⵜⵥⵠ kdi, to desire, to require, to gain .

kdi, duty .

Q

ⵍ q, act .

q, desires ;

ⵞⵍ **q-ne** yearning , producing .

ⵢⵍ qe, make .

qe, renewal , creation ; **qe-ne** creator.

Heq qe-ne, existence .

Eqeq qeqe, a super creation

Nq qn, he acts .

ⵞⵥ.VIIIⵍ qo<u>sn</u>-ne, Kushites .

ⵜⵍ qi, life .

ⵥⵍ qn, knows, understand .

Iⵍ qo, to live, to be renewed, restore .

ധዓ₭ or, monarch .

ᖇധዓ₭ qor-o, respectable, virtuous, worshipful, lordly .

T

ꓥ t, here .

-t, you, your .

t, arrange .

ና2ꓥ t-ne, the good.

ⰷና2ꓥ tak, reflection .

ﾚꓥ tb, proclaim; ┼ﾚꓥ **tb-i** disclosure, dissemination, spreading
    abroad

┼ꓥ ti, go arrange

ꝫꓥ tm, to be born, bear, come into the world; **tm-o** open the
    rebirth.

⫽⫽ና3ꓥ tmey, give form to the rebirth

₭ꓥ tq, to set in motion .

ና2ናᢕ┼ꓥ timhene, he goes grandly to direct .

ᢕꓥ th, move ??? .

ⰷꓥ tk, to be, to investigate, to move, to reflect .

    tk, set in motion .

ᖆꓥ tn, the rebirth .

ധꓥ tr, to raise, to erect, to support .

/ʊʒ tr-o, elevation, eminence, prominence .

/4ʒ t<u>s</u>, the commandant, chief .

x7 t<u>n</u>, the rebirth , t<u>n</u>-ne 'rebirth' .

.

To

ɤ to, to kindle, excite, ignite, burning ; ૬2ɤ to-ne

vigorousness ,dynamicism, energy, physical fitness ,

combustion;vigorous .

ɤ to, light, fire .

૬2ɤ tone, the rebirth .

T^e

/4 t^e, your, you ;(2) he.

૬2Ⴑ/4 t^e<u>n</u>-a, come into being.te, to put, to lay .

/4 t^e, this, the .

t^e, towards, where, may (it go forth) .

V/4 t^{e}b, loftiness .

$/4 t^{e}l, lift, rise, elevate, raise .

૬2$/4 t^{e}l-ne, erection, elevation, ascent, loftiness .

ᒪ/4 t^{e}p, announce in a lofty voice .

$/4 t^{e}m, rebirth, beget, be born reborn .

૬2/4 t^{e}ne, the rebirth, to the rebirth .

tᵉne, to arrange .

+w/4 tᵉri, fashion.

D

𝔷 **d**, leave a legacy, confer, convey, deed, transfer .

𝔔𝔷 **d-ne**, transmission, deliver, bequest, pledge, inheritance .

𝔷 **d**, indeed .

  d, bequeath, donate .

𝔔𝔷 **d-ne**, bequeathal, donations .

𝔷𝔷 **d-d**, (use of reduplication) considerable donat(ions) .

𝔷 **de**, offerings; **de-b** much offerings .

/4𝔷 **detᵉ**, your donation/ almsgiving.

𝔷 **de**, indeed .

𝔷 **dl**, rising.

/𝔷 **do**, to be , to lead .

+𝔷 **di**, for its passage .

ℝ𝔷 **dn**, to come into the world, to bear, to produce .

Appendix 1: Candace Amanirenas

Candace Amanirenas

Meroitic-Kush never became part of the Roman empire – although the Romans tried to make it part. In 24 B.C., the Romans were planning a campaign against both Meroitic-Kush (Meroë) and Arabia.

Augustus (31 BC-14 AD), when he defeated Mark Antony and Cleopatra, got control of Egypt. He made it a Roman province, governed by an equestrian prefect under his own control. Kush – just to Egypt's south – was outside the empire.

In 24 B.C. Roman forces were sent to fight in Arabia. According to Pliny and Strabo the Meroite-Kushites sacked Aswan and destroyed the Roman statues at Philae (Török, 1998; Welsby, 1996).

In response to the Kushite expedition, Gaius Petronius with a force of 10,000 infantry and 800 horses pushed the Kushites back to Pselchis. Strabo (17.1.53) mentions the fact that the Meroites were led by a Candace and her son Akinidad.

The Romans and Kushites, according to Strabo began peace negotiations at Dakka in 24 B.C.. The negotiations failed, and the Romans pushed their forces deeper into Meroitic-Kushite territory as far as Sara. They also established forts at Qasr Ibrim (Török, 1998; Welsby, 1996).

Akinidad was probably killed in 24 B.C. Strabo (17.1.54) mentions that the Candace's son was killed during this campaign. This son of the Candance was probably Akinidad.

We know that Akinidad was in Dakka on two occasions, once with Teriteqas, and later only with Amanirenas. In Dakka 2, we discover that Akinidad died at Dakka. This is most interesting because, the Romans pushed the Meroites back to Dakka in 24 B.C.

If Akinidad had been wounded outside Dakka, Amanirenas may have stopped in the town to obtain medical treatment for her son. After Akinidad died in the town, Amanirenas may have withdrawn from peace talks and continued the War.

If these events occurred , Amanirenas probably had the Qasr Ibrim 1420 stela erected in Qasr Ibrim, to honor Akinidad who had served as the Chief of the city during the Meroitic-Roman War. The Qasr Ibrim 1420 stela was probably defaced and broken during the Roman occupation of Qasr Ibrim to show their contempt for the Meroites.

The Meroites resisted Roman occupation. By 22 B.C., the Meroites retook Qasr Ibrim from the Romans. In 21 B.C., a peace treaty was concluded between Augustus, and Meroite envoys on the Island of Samos.

The textual evidence makes it clear that Akinidad remained a paqar (prince) until his death at Dakka in 24 B.C.

The evidence of the Dakka 2 inscription and Hamadab 2 indicate that Akinidad probably died during Amanirenas rule of Merotic-Kush. After Teriteqas was killed during the Meroitic-Roman War, Akinidad may have become recognized as King, but without official

succession, and his untimely death at Dakka, he remained until his death officially Crown Prince. This would explain our inability to find any evidence of Akinidad being recognized as anything more than a paqar, rather than a qore (king).

Two large stela bearing the name Akinidad from the Hamdab temple, is the funerary stela of Kharapkhael, the older brother of Akinidad. In this stela Akinidad described as a paqar (prince). This suggest that Kharapkhael was the original crown prince, not Akinidad of King Teriteqas and Queen Amanirenas.

It has usually been considered that Amanirenas was Greek geographer Strabo's "Candace".

During battle, the Candace lost an eye; but this only made her more courageous. "One Eyed Candace," as then Roman governor Gaius Petronius referred to her.

The Meroitic-Kush kingdom would last as long as the western Roman empire did – until the fifth century, when a new kingdom

End Notes

1. The term **Pesto** is very interesting. In Egyptian **pesto** means 'King's son'. In Meroitic **pesto** signifies '(he) who vouchsafes the king's light' or 'the king's foundation of light'. It is composed of three words **pe** 'vouchsafe; foundation', **s** 'king' and **to** 'light'.

2. This **-t,** is the suffix used to form preterit pronouns.

3. This **-i,** is the particle used to form verbs into adjectives.

4. The -n particle is used to form the third personal pronoun.

5. This term **h,** or **Kha** is the abstract personality of man.

6. **Bane,** may be related to the **Ba** of Egyptian religion. The **Ba,** united the conception of the **Kha** and the **Kho** 'the translucent spirit soul. **Bane,** was probably the place where these spirits dwell after death if they left the grave. The object of these obituaries were probably aimed at getting the dead to settle in **Bane,** rather than hunt the grave.

7. This **-a** particle was used to form the future tense.

8. This **-m** particle was used in Meroitic to form the verb to be.

9. This is the Meroitic **-a** subjunctive used to form the future tense.

10. This is use of the **-a** suffix to form the third person pronoun 'he,her,it'.

11. Here we see the use of reduplication to form the plural. Here we has **an** **'life spirit'**, **an an** therefore would mean **'considerable life spirit'**.

12.This is the use of -**b,** to form the plural in Meroitic.

13.Here we see again the use of reduplication to form the plural number **d ne**'good donation'; **d d ne** 'considerable donation'.

14. Here we see use of the -n particle, which was used to form the subjunctive when joined to Meroitic verbs to make the future tense.

15.Here and later in this same passage we see use of the particle -m, which was used to show the third person tense.

16.Here we see the **-a** particle used to form the plural number in Meroitic words e.g., **bk-ne** 'perfection', **bk-ne-a** 'much perfection'.

17. The reference here to Bes, appears to indicate that Kharapkhael died at a relatively young age. This results from the fact that Bes, is the god of childbirth , and may have been implored in this text by Amanirenas to protect her young child on his way to paradise.

Made in the USA
Middletown, DE
09 July 2015